Christmas In America

Olimpia Monrroy Ochoa

BookLeaf Publishing

Presentation by *BookLeaf Publishing*

Web: www.bookleafpub.com

E-mail: info@bookleafpub.com

ISBN: 9789357215015

First edition 2022

The Origin of Presents

It all began a long time ago,
When half the world would be covered in snow.
Times were simple, hard, and unkind,
But we somehow found the joy in life.
The meaning of Christmas was different back then,
All that mattered was a baby in a pen.
The origin of chaos started with three generous men.
Unknowingly starting a whole world of mess.
They each brought a gift for the baby king,
Riding on a camel, horse, and donkey.
The rest of the world adopted their kindness,
For centuries to come there would be madness.
We filled the season with material things,
Some going as far as becoming selfish.
We are not content with garland and sweets,
All that matters in the latest new thing.
Long gone are the days of company being enough,
We all want phones, tablets, and fluff.
But we need to remember when it all started from,
A baby, a manger, and a boy with a drum.

Christmas Hell

Mariah n' Celine playing on repeat.
Swarms of people with no Christmas cheer.
No space for parking.
The bills keep climbing.
This holiday season brings me to tears.

The Anatomy of a Christmas Tree

Wood Brown Scratchy Green
Forest Needle Cuts Sting
Sparkle Lights Glass Silver
Fruit Flowers Snow Tinsel
Elf Train Bulb Car
Bows Bell Bear Star

A Far Away Christmas

I will never forget my last Christmas there.
It seems so close, yet so far away.
Maybe it's the pictures, or stories being told.
But I will never forget the feeling of old.
When the whole family gathered, the old and the young,
It is impossible to believe eighteen years have gone by.
How can it be that we miss what never was?
The food, the traditions, the people, and mas.
I yearned to be included in the grown-up exchange,
What a silly thing to miss, life is now changed.
There are now people missing, faces you don't know,
The next generation is old and all grown.
All these years I wished to go back,
It took a long time to realize that,
The Christmases here have not been all bad.
They have been filled with joy, laughter, and a man in a hat.
Traditions evolve, family grows bigger.
You meet new people who always deliver,
A feeling of home, belonging, a laugh, and a giggle.

To The Children:

Twinkle in your eyes.
Don’t let the world turn you cold.
Remember, be nice!

The Twelve Days of Christmas

Everyone complains how Christmas goes too fast, but the twelve days before can be such a blast.
Not everything must be done all at once, why don't we take some time to discuss.
The first day of Christmas is for putting up the tree, with garland, lights, and tinsel, you see.
The second day you can treat yourself, by watching a movie about a snowman and elf.
The next thing to do is build a gingerbread house, make it delicious, watch out for the mouse.
On the fourth day, if the weather is nice you can go caroling or skating on ice.
An apple pie can be made of the fifth, just make sure you get Granny Smith's.
The sixth can be used to learn reindeer names.
Donner and Rudolph, they love playing games.
On the seventh day take another pause to look at Christmas lights just because.
Getting gifts for your family and friends, better hurry before the sales end.

The ninth and tenth day are for wrapping presents and drinking hot cocoa which is always so pleasant.
Don’t forget on the eleventh day to take some time to give thanks and pray.
The last thing to do on Christmas Eve night is to make cookies for Santa and his wife.

Noche Buena

Para empezar el dia tenemos que limpiar
El carro, la casa y también afuera.
Vamos a la tienda para comprar
Todos los ingredientes para cenar.
Tamales, pozole, champurrado, y ponche
Son unas de las cosas que comemos esa noche.
Después nos arreglamos con rojo y verde,
Plata y oro para la buena suerte.
Comemos, cantamos, bailamos, reímos,
Y a la media noche acostamos al niño.

The Truth About the Reindeer

I will now shed some truth on Santa's reindeer.
They all have their quirks just like you and me,
dear.
Dasher is constantly late, never being on time.
Prancer is known for being a clutz.
Dancer can't keep still, always moving.
Cupid and Vixen just keep on flirting.
Comet can't keep his hoofs on the ground.
Donner is so glad Rudolph's around.
Blitzen in the corral passed out drunk.
Those are the reindeer, a whole bunch of punks.

A Letter to Santa

Dear Santa,
It has been some years since I have written to you.
I am much older now, though still in my youth.
Though I am sure I've been naughty, I've tried to be nice,
I really would love it if you could comply.
Let's start off with some materials things,
Though they are not as important, they are things I need.
Please give me a job, shelter, and food,
Or maybe a gas card would be good too.
Now let's move on to the things that are valuable,
All the things that aren't programmable.
Those would be mother, father, sister, and dogs,
Birds, partners, friends, the whole lot.
Please give us happiness, joy and health
That's all I need for the year to be swell!

SANTA CLAUS

Somewhere in the North Pole
All red suit made of velvet
Nice round belly
Twinkle in his eyes
Ability to make a whole bunch of toys

Cookie crumbs on his beard
Loves the spirit of the world
Always nice to his wife and elves
Up all night flying around
Singing jingle all the way

If

Oh to be Santa and fly through the night
To make people happy and smile real bright,
To not think of I, or me, or we,
If we weren't so selfish how great would it be?

Mrs. Claus' Night

Every now and then we should thank Mrs. Claus
For sharing her husband on such a special night.
She understands the great responsibility he has
And does not greet him by starting a fight.
To pass the time she puts on some jazz
While making a drink with fruit punch and
sprite.
She has a great party full of pizzaz
Awaiting her husband with a smile all bright.

Christmas Resolution

Watching the tree twinkling aglow,
It makes me relieved the year's almost gone.
Each year time passes slightly faster,
feels like life is becoming a disaster.
People are fighting all over the globe,
and me in the house with food and cocoa.
We need to be grateful for all that we have,
And try to be more like the ol' man Santa.

The Meaning of Christmas

Remove all the light, the presents, the tree,
I wonder how many of use would see,
The value of Christmas and holidays,
A time to be spent with family and friends.

The Christmas Bear

I like polar bears, yes I do.
They are just like me and you.
All the mommas take care of their babies.
And just like us they can get rabies.
They love to eat fish, berries, and meat.
They are not fans of eating some beets.
And though they are scary, with teeth that are sharp.
They are my favorite, they flutter my heart.

The First Christmas

The first Christmas after you have left
the nest
is always odd.
You are finally able to
decorate how you wish,
do the activities you want to,
not have to be on anybody else's timeline.
But you know what is funny?
We still resort to those family
traditions
that has been done for years.
We cannot escape them,
and we don't want to.
We want to keep them alive,
share them,
pass them on.
There is guilt attached too,
you are doing fun activities often without them.
Like putting up lights.
Decorating the tree.
Cookies.
Gingerbread houses.
Christmas cards.
Wrapping presents.
Christmas music.

If you are lucky you might have someone beside you to do them with
If you are extra lucky you might call the family you left to do Christmas with you.

Poinsettias

The Christmas flower, the beautiful poinsettia,
In spanish we call her la bonita noche buena.
She brings us success, luck, and good cheer,
All things that are needed for the upcoming year.

The Next Day

I wonder what happens December 26th,
If Santa, and Frosty, and elves, and reindeer,
They gather around with food and good drinks,
And proudly rejoice the end of the year.

Some Day in Between

The year's almost over, we've had a good run.
There's been highs and lows, and lots of great fun.
May we never forget the lessons we learned,
And be grateful for the fruits that were well earned.
Wishing everyone a happy new year,
Hoping granted wishes for you are near.

New Year's Eve Eve

Preparing for the end of the year is quite
bittersweet,
I wish I could be outside on mainstreet.
Not worried about the troubles of past,
or the troubles ahead that haven't been cast.
Can't figure out if it's better alone,
in some little town that is full of snow.
Or where you can see the city at night,
surrounded by people with phones and lights.
It is better with family, and friends, and our pets,
They are with us all year long, and you can wear
sweats.

Grape Wishes

I wish for the same twelve things every night,
While eating grapes and drinking champán.
I wish for my health, and maybe some wealth.
For momma, papa, and siblings as well.
I hope that the pets stay with us one more year,
Or perhaps adopt one to bring us more cheer.
May my lover be full of peace and of glee,
and hoping I eat some extra veggies.
If I'm quite honest, for the last three,
Already having enough, I chew them carefree.

www.ingramcontent.com/pod-product-compliance
Lightning Source LLC
Chambersburg PA
CBHW051721130826
49812CB00034B/1285
9789357215015